Titles by Janvier Chouteu-Chando

The Usurper: and Other Stories
Triple Agent, Double Cross
Disciples of Fortune
The Union Moujik
Splendid Comets
Flash of the Sun
Fortune Calls
Fortune's Master
Fortune's Children
The Norilsk Bears
To Be In Love and To Be Wise
The Fire and Ice Legend
The Sweetest Madness
The Grandmothers
The Hunger Fire
The Shades of Fire
Father and Sons
The Doctors
Dark Shades
Fateful Ties
The Verdict of Hades
His Majesty's Trial
Ngoko's Folly
The Usurper
The Dowry
I am Hated
The Oaf

Non-Fiction Titles by Janvier Chouteu-Chando

THE CANARY IN A COAL MINE EFFECT:...Assassinations...
THEIR LAST STAND: Donald Trump's Upset Victory…
BROKEN ENGAGEMENT: Why a Donald Trump Win…
Ukraine: The Tug-of-war between Russia and the West
Cameroon: The Haunted Heart of Africa

The Bamileké Factor
in the Cause for the New Cameroon: and Other Articles

The Successful Century-Old Divide-and-Rule Policy in Africa Brought About by the Creation of a Virtual Enemy Within

Janvier Tchouteu

TISI BOOKS

NEW YORK, RALEIGH, LONDON, AMSTERDAM

The Bamileké Factor in the Cause for the New Cameroon:
and Other Articles
    Copyright © 2017 by Janvier Tchouteu

ISBN-13: 978-1-7179-2820-7
ISBN-10:   1-7179-2820-X

PUBLISHED BY TISI BOOKS
www.tisibooks.com

NEW YORK, RALEIGH, LONDON, AMSTERDAM

Printed in The United States of America

EPIGRAPH

"The time for revolutionaries with the complete freedom to maneuver is over."
—CHRISTOPHER NKWAYEP-CHANDO

DEDICATION

This collection is dedicated to the loving memory of my maternal grandmother's mother (great-grandmother) Yam Ngan.

ACKNOWLEDGMENTS

My deepest, warmest and everlasting thanks to Dr. Samuel F. Tchwenko and Christopher N. Chando for challenging me towards the path of humanity's enhancement.

The Bamileké Factor

in the Cause for the New Cameroon: and Other Articles

The Successful Century-Old Divide-and-Rule Policy in Africa Brought About by the Creation of a Virtual Enemy Within

Contents

MAPS

African Democracy Ratings

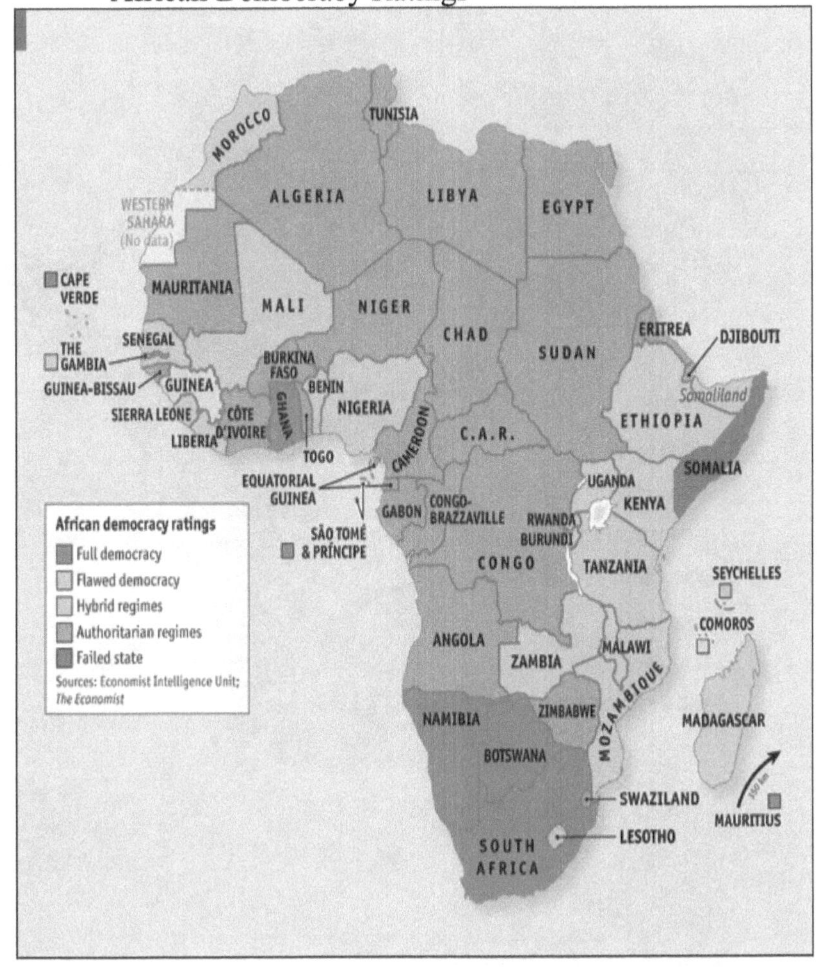

Partition Map of Africa: 1884-1914

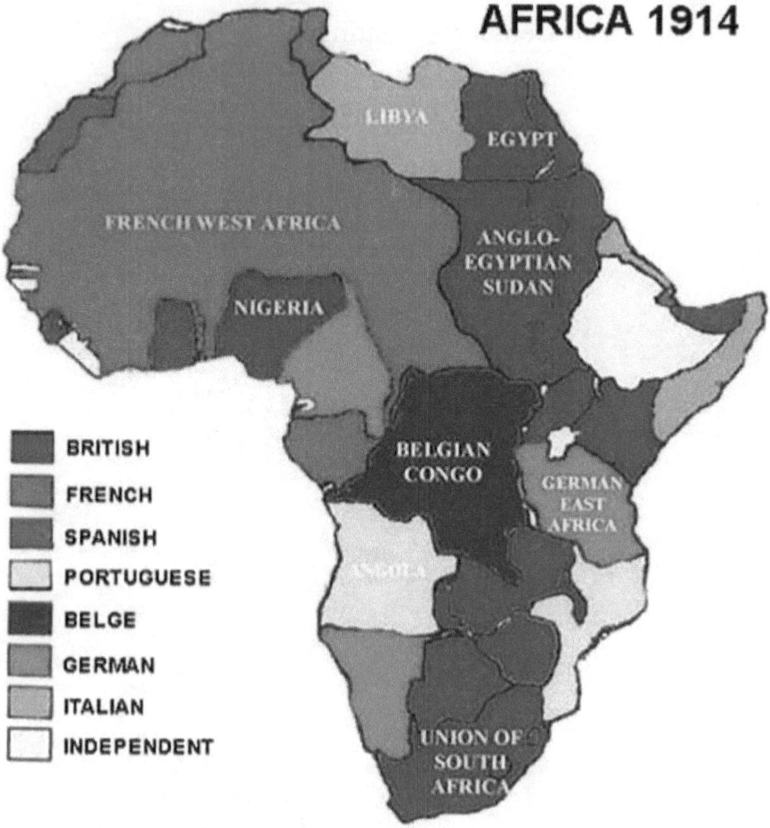

Cameroon on a map of the world

Cameroon over time

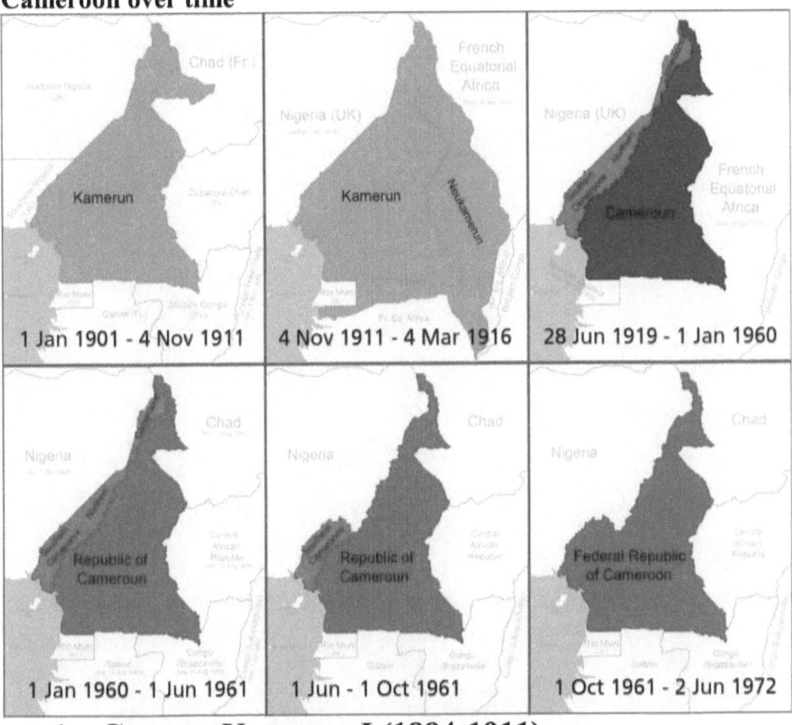

1. **German Kamerun I (1884-1911)**
2. **German Kamerun II (1911-1916)**
3. **British Cameroons&French Cameroun: 1916-1960**
4. **British Cameroons&La Republique du Cameroun (1960-1961)**
5. **British Southern Cameroons&La Republique du Cameroun (1960-1961)**
6. **Reunited/Independent Cameroon today.**

Chapter One

THE BAMILEKÉ FACTOR IN THE CAMEROONIAN STRUGGLE

Understanding mass psychology should be the strength of any leader striving to alleviate the pains and miseries of the masses, especially in a multi-ethnic and multi-cultural nation like Cameroon.

Bamilekés, Bamilekés, Bamilekés. Looking at Bamilekés with the eyes of those non-Bamileké people who have never understood them, Bamilekés are sometimes subjected to suspicion, envy and to point hatred. To most of the non-Bamilekés who came close to Bamilekés and understood the pattern of their collective psyche, they are perhaps Cameroon's most trusted or one of its most trusted and reliable ethnic groups, the people most of the nation's other ethnic groups can turn to first in times of difficulties and find solace. Bamilekés easily relate.

But who are the Bamilekés and what are they to themselves in the complex political arena that is Cameroon? They are a traumatized people; still traumatized by the UPC war against French and Ahidjo forces. In a partisan war of liberation under the UPC leadership of Ruben Um Nyobé, an ethnic Bassa (1956-1958), they were steadfast in their commitment to the struggle; when Felix

Moumié, an ethnic Bamoun (1958-1960) took over the UPC leadership after Um Nyobé's assassination, the Bamilekés continued fighting with most of the other Francophone Cameroonian ethnic groups; when Ernest Ouandjie-Bamileké took over in 1960 after Moumié 's assassination by thallium poisoning in Geneva by William Bechtel, an agent of the French secret service, the Bamilekés stayed on course. By 1962, most of the leaders of the other ethnic factions of the UPC had either been defeated, killed, exiled or had reneged and joined the French puppet Ahidjo government, leaving the Bamilekés continuing a war where they lost more than half of their population in the Bamilekéland. It was a bitter lesson, which culminated in the execution of Ernest Ouandjie in 1971 after he gave himself up to the Ahidjo regime in order to stop the massacre of his people. During 1960-1970, was born a stereotype that haunts Bamilekés and other Cameroonians until today, a stereotype effectively planted into the minds of Cameroonians by the French-imposed system and the Ahidjo regime (They—the Bamilekés have economic power, and now, they also want political power).

Many Cameroonians failed to understand that the Bamilekés got involved in the genuine nationalist cause for the liberation of Cameroon under Um Nyobé at the time because they believed in Cameroonian nationalism and stayed on course after others had deserted because they are steadfast by nature and consider surrender to a right cause as undignified, dishonorable and a betrayal.

The mass Bamileké psychology: They know what they do not want, but they have not mastered how to get what they want in the general Cameroonian context that is so complex. True they are the most nationalistic group in the country. It is true that despite having about 30% of the population, they have shown their preparedness to massively back any broad-based national endeavor even if it is not led by a Bamileké, especially if the endeavor rallies other ethnic groups to the national goals of the Cameroonian struggle.

It has been observed with clarity that the Bamileké masses know that they do not want the Biya regime. Still, there are Bamileké elites in the French-imposed system which is France's biggest political mafia setup in Africa. These Bamilekés are like other collaborators that you will find from all the ethnic groups of this land. Yes, collaborators are to be found in every retrogressive system, and in Cameroon, we have them from all the ethnic groups.

It has also been observed with clarity that the SDF leadership under Fru Ndi betrayed the all-embracing ideals of Cameroonian Union-Nationalism, which Bamilekés joined the SDF believing that the Fru Ndi-led SDF shared. And truly, the national agenda of the struggle espoused by most Cameroonians and most Bamilekés dominated the SDF from 1990-1997, making the SDF a historic party during that period. During the difficult years of the struggle, some three-quarters of SDF's funding came from Bamilekés, with figures like Kadji Defosso leading in most of the efforts. But Fru Ndi's mafia in the SDF betrayed the all-embracing trust built in the party as the clique started pursuing an exclusive agenda that many of the first founders had in mind before the party got swamped by Cameroonian nationalists late in 1990, thereby leaving the Union-Nationalist faction of the SDF where most Bamilekés belonged exposed. It became clear that the difficult path to realizing the change of the system was no longer possible under Fru Ndi's idea of the SDF that he had deceived most in the Northwest province and the rest of Cameroon to believe in. And like a slap in the face, the memories of the 1962-1970 genocide came to mind.

Some say the vast majority of the Bamileké population has matured politically and knows that their best interest rests in a new Cameroon where all the ethnic groups have a stake in it; that this majority knows that they have to work with other ethnic groups to realize that change. But then, a dilemma looms. They had followed unbending and genuine nationalists like Um Nyobé and Felix Moumié who were not of Bamileké origin and were inspired by them; They followed Fru Ndi who later proved that he was not genuine in his intentions and betrayed them; They know that the French-imposed system and the Biya regime does not have their interest at heart and should never be supported; and yet they know that the last time a Bamileké leader (Ernest Ouandjie) led the struggle, some of the leaders of other ethnic groups convinced their populations to desert the historic UPC of 1948-1970 through lies that Bamilekés stand to completely dominate the country if the UPC were to make it to political power because that would add on top of their economic lead. This divide-and-rule strategy was of course devised by Jacques Foccart, French president Charles De Gaulle's strategist on Africa who did an amazing job of presenting the national revolt by the UPC as a 1962 ethnic revolt by the Bamilekés.

My conclusion is that this country will never change unless Cameroonians come to terms with their brainwashed past and reject the stereotyping that was created by the system on the Anglophone and Bamileké populations especially. During the good days of the SDF, most Cameroonians came to terms with the Anglophone factor, which saw Fru Ndi deriving more Francophone support than any other political leader. But the sad thing is that when Fru Ndi and his clique were cornered to account for the party's derailment, they stirred Bamileké phobia as a way out of his failures, thereby undermining the struggle and misinforming the population, which has resulted in the rising anti-Bamilekéism in some political circles within certain parts of the Anglophone population. The consequence is that it has destroyed the trust that had been built over the years in the grand West of Cameroon under the banner of the SDF.

Janvier Tchouteu   *August 2004*

Afterthought:

In this fourth phase of the struggle that began on October 10, 2011, Cameroon risks spending more years in the political, economic and social wilderness while less privileged African nations with a sense of direction forge ahead in the race towards progress, democracy, human rights and higher living standards. Cameroon as a nation will be stuck in inertia if we as individuals or collectively fail to reject the stereotypes perpetuated by the evil system and if we fail to embrace one another in the collective struggle to found THE NEW CAMEROON. It is impossible to do that without killing the anti-Bamilekéism we have within.

11/15/2011

Chapter Two

ANTI-BAMILEKÉISM AS A RETARDING ELEMENT IN THE STRUGGLE FOR A NEW CAMEROON

I have seen purported exponents of change in Cameroon expressing themselves with blinding emotions against an entire people; without doing themselves the favor of rereading their write-ups—a process that works best if they pretend for a moment that they are not the writer. That is the surest way of cultivating objectivity, the easiest path to get an idea of how others will perceive your write up.

It defies logic when these so-called exponents of change hold strong anti-Bamileké sentiments against an entire people who are in their overwhelming majority in rejecting the evil system in power. Why they reserve the hardest and most discriminatory language for these opponents of the system who have embraced an ideology based on Cameroonian Union-Nationalism, you, I and others can figure that out. They have been deformed by the system and left with the legacy of a twisted mindset that embraced the divide-and-rule strategy hatched by Jacques Foccart, a strategy aimed at making the Bamileké ethnic group the national scapegoat, and presenting it to the rest of Cameroonians as the national enemy within, all in the bid to maintain and perpetuate French unfettered control in Cameroon. Now, to the poisoned minds, it is as if the

Bamileké people are more of an enemy than the evil system in power. Unbiased advocates of change can best explain the irrationality of these biased minds or their consumption by blinding or negative emotions by analyzing the motives of the anachronistic French-imposed system managed in Cameron today by the Biya regime for the interest of special groups in France.

It is illogical or even criminal to judge a person based on his/her ethnic group, because all ethnic groups in Cameroon would draw blinding emotions or preconceptions from other Cameroonians who think in the light of collectivizing blame and hate. There are always people out there who have had bad experiences with a Fulani, Bamileké, Duala, Bakwerian, Beti, Makaa, Bayang, Batanga,Bassa, Tikar, Bamoun,Ngambay, Gbaya, Voko, Gidar, Kotoko, Bakossi, Bali, Ngemba, Massa, Kapsiki, etc person and used that experience to condemn the entire people of that group or tribe. Xenophobia, ethnocentrism, ethnic cleansing and genocide are usually born from that mindset.

The vast majority of Germans three generations after are still haunted by that era of Nazism and the treatment of the Jews, and regret it deeply; yet we have Cameroonians who purport to be exponents of change and at the same time, try to apportion some rationale or justification to the Nazi-inspired and executed hatred.

I will not dwell lengthily on this distraction of anti-Bamileké sentiments coming from people who are engaged in a cause but cannot identify their real enemies.

In the 1995 article "HOW COMMITTED ARE WE IN THE STRUGGLE TO CHANGE THE PRESENT SYSTEM", I stated that exponents of change who think that way belong with the category called the confused and one-sided...

"The third force are the confused and one-sided who are fervently fighting for causes that do not address the general Cameroonian plight, but rather address the plight of an ethnic group, religious belief, region or linguistic entity. The fact that they are deeply attached to their belief in the righteousness of their cause, and the fact that they consider all those who are not fully behind them as their enemies; this confused and one-sided force for change (which by their demands call for partiality), not only alienate themselves from potential allies for change, but also alienate themselves from the general objectives of the Cameroonian struggle which encompasses their plight. And in a curious way without them really knowing it, they stall the wind of change because of their divisive actions and directions."

Anti-Bamilekéism is something I too experienced firsthand as an exponent of change in the SDF (Social Democratic Front) from 1990-2002, on several occasions actually. It is one of the system's cancers implanted in the minds of many Cameroonians that is haunting this nation today. It played a major role in breaking the carefully-crafted cooperation between the different forces in the SDF and led to the pathetic state of the party today. It also affected the UPC (Union of the Populations of the Cameroons) partisan movement during its last years. Exponents of change will never change the system while anti-Bamilekéism and Anglophobia exist in its leadership. Thank God the vast majority of the Cameroonian people east and west of the River Mungo do not see a problem being an Anglophone, even though the French-imposed system is uncomfortable about it. But it is disheartening when one is forced to observe the morbid expression of anti-Bamilekéism from people who purport to be against the system and who especially come from ranks that have been discriminated upon by the evil system in power.

Hate groups like Hamas killed more Palestinians fighting Israel than Israelis they purported to be out to eliminate. Taliban killed more Mujahideen (Islamic fighters) than others who did not share their extremist views. The Nazis killed their Jews, even those who fought in the German army during the First World War. Those advocating blinding emotions of hate end up destroying themselves. That phenomenon abounds in history.

We cannot afford to confront the evil system in the next phase of the struggle with divided ranks.

Janvier Tchouteu   *January 15, 2009*

Chapter Three

ANTI-BAMILEKÉ SENTIMENTS AND CAMEROON'S UNION-NATIONALISM

Hate is a negative and blinding emotion. And there is a name for a disease that affects people who hate or are fearful of those people or things they shouldn't be hateful or afraid of. It is called Persecution Mania.

I indicated decades ago after a careful observation, that Cameroonians may never be able to muster the full strength to get rid of the French-imposed system unless they come to terms with their Anglophone and Bamileké problems. The majority of Cameroonians (Francophone and Anglophones, with the exception of the minority system in power) came to terms with the Anglophone problem and voted in their majority for Fru Ndi, an Anglophone, just like the majority of Americans overcame centuries-and-decades-old biases over blacks by voting Obama into power.

But it saddens me when individuals who come from the Anglophone group who have been marginalized by the system, blatantly exhibit those same biases and preconceptions against an ethnic group—-the Bamilekés. Using fear or hatred of the Bamilekés especially, was one of the major rallying cries that the French, Ahidjo and the system at large used to maintain their stay in power. We thought that preconception of the Bamilekés as a national enemy within had been broken in 1990. It appears it has not been broken.

We can never beat the system unless we overcome the Bami, Anglo and other group brainwashings that was made the mindset by the system in power. Anybody who keeps rattling about it makes himself or herself an enemy of the people and an obstacle to change. You automatically put yourself as a dividing force in the struggle.

The historical forces are close to the configuration that will sweep the system out of power. We cannot afford to have divided ranks at that historic moment. Our future should belong with a democratic, united, economically integrated Africa; our future should be A New Cameroon that guarantees civil rights, liberties, and benefits for its population. Cameroon would be the epitome of that new Africa as an embodiment of the positive results that can come out of a diverse people with a tragic past; who overcame their traumas and differences, harnessed their hopes and dreams and built on their mutual compatibilities to realize a successful nation-state.

Our generation has the colossal task of realizing Cecil Rhode's vision of a railway line from Cape Town to Cairo, and to draw from Africa's contemporary unifying heroes in the unavoidable path that will culminate in Africa's economic union and political integration. To achieve those goals, we have to look beyond our noses.

A true Cameroonian nationalist of the union bent (Union nationalist) does not dwell on ethnicity, tribe, linguistic affiliation, or religion etc. The union nationalists with the revolutionary vision won't even subject themselves to the mercy or handout of the system, its backers or those who out of personal interest are dealing or collaborating with the system.

I don't think I am alone in looking forward to a future where an African would say *Ubi bebe, ibi patria vera*! (Where it goes well with me, there is my true fatherland.), or where I would say I am a Bakwerian born Cameroonian or a South West born Bamileké; without receiving snorting replies to my pronouncements. Or even be called Mola, just like some of my father's friends always called him.

Let a thousand ideas flourish on how the future, accepting and enriching New Cameroon should look like. Cameroon has a historic role to play in realizing the New Africa. The carelessly drawn triangle many of us fondly refer to as Pays embodies Africa's spirit.

No people are collectively evil. Only individuals are evil. And the evil system in place has elements from all the religious, ethnic and social groupings in Cameroon. The Germans were never collectively condemned as bloodthirsty despite the atrocities of Nazism. The Hutus were not ostracized over the Rwandan genocide. All Rwandans today are viewed as potential builders of the New Rwanda, a country that stands in Africa as one of the few in Africa that has a sense of direction.

So, advocates of the New Cameroon, Union Nationalists of all shades of ideas and beliefs; Let's join hands in rejecting the system, confronting it and working for the foundation and development of the NEW CAMEROON that rejects the stereotypes hatched by Jacques Foccart and the anti-Cameroonian system put in place by France, a system that is stifling our development and dividing our ranks.

Janvier Tchouteu   *10/13/2010*

GLOSSARY ON CAMEROON

<u>*(Excerpt of "Triple Agent, Double Cross")*</u>

Adamawa | The southernmost province that was carved out of the former Grand North Province. It is a plateau region.

Akonolinga | A town in the Center Region. It is also the capital of the Nyong and Nfomou Division.

Akum | A Ngemba settlement 9 miles from Bamenda along the Bafoussam-Bamenda road. It is also a traditional Ngemba kingdom and the dialect of the people there.

Ambam | A town in the South Region. It is a sub-divisional capital in Ntem Division.

Ashia | Word used by both English and French-speaking Cameroonians to express sympathy, condolence, consolation, encouragement, compassion, harmony, understanding, agreement, thankfulness, and caution.

Bafang — The capital of Upper Nkam Division and a Bamileké kingdom in the West Region.

Bafaw — The principal ethnic group in the area that comprises the Kumba municipality. It is part of the larger Bantu group.

Bafedja — A settlement and Bamileké kingdom in the Nde or Banganté Division, West Region.

Bafoussam — The capital of the West Region and Mifi Division. Also a traditional Bamileké kingdom.

Bafut — A settlement and traditional Ngemba kingdom about 18 miles from Bamenda in the Northwest Region.

Bakweri — The principal ethnic group in the Fako Division, which is located in the Southwest Region. The Bakwerians are Bantu speaking of the Sawabantu subgroup.

Balengou	Bamileké settlement and kingdom in the Nde Division, West Region.
Bali	A Chamba settlement and kingdom about 18 miles north of Bamenda, in the Northwest Region.
Bamena	Bamileké settlement and kingdom in the Nde Division, West Region.
Bambili	A settlement and Ngemba kingdom about 9 miles north of Bamenda in the Northwest Region.
Bambui	A Ngemba settlement and kingdom about 6 miles north of Bamenda in the Northwest Region.
Bamenda	The capital of the Northwest Region and Mezam Division.
Bamendjou	Bamileké settlement and kingdom in the Mifi Division, West Region.
Bami (Bamileké)	Diminutive of Bamileké.
Bamileké (Bami)	The most populous semi-Bantu ethnicity and the principal ethnic group in Cameroon. It is also their

mother tongue.

Bamilekéland   The western half of the West Region, with fringes in the Northwest and Southwest Regions. It comprises five administrative divisions, about ninety traditional kingdoms, and eleven dialectical groupings.

Bamoun   A semi-Bantu ethnicity and one of the principal ethnic groups in Cameroon. Also their mother tongue.

Bamounland   The Eastern half of the Western province.

Bandekop   A Bamileké settlement and kingdom in Mifi Division, West Region.

Banganté   The largest Bamileké kingdom, the capital of Nde Division, its former name. Found in the West Region.

Bangou   A Bamileké settlement and kingdom in the Upper Nkam Division, West Region.

Bangoua   Bamileké settlement and kingdom in Nde Division, West Region.

Bangoulap	Bamileké settlement and kingdom in Nde Division, West Region.
Bantu	A Large group of Negroid peoples of Central, South, and East Africa that inhabits the forests of the Southwest, Littoral, Center, South, and East Regions of Cameroon. Also the largest constituent of the Negroid or Black race.
Bassa	The principal ethnic group in the Littoral Region. It is Bantu speaking. Also found in the Center Region of Cameroon.
Batoufam	Bamileké kingdom in the Mifi Division, West Region.
Bawok (Bahouok, Bahouoc)	Bamileké kingdoms speaking the Medumba dialects, found in the West and Northwest Regions. The principal ones are:

- Bawok-Banganté or Banganté-Bawok is a traditional Bamileké kingdom found in the Banganté subdivision, Nde Division. Much of the kingdom is located in the city of Banganté. Following a series of strives in the early twentieth century, it lost most of its territory to the surrounding Bamileké kingdoms, with its subjects migrating to other areas in Cameroon and even founding new kingdoms.

- Bawok-Bali or Bali-Bawok: An offshoot of the mother kingdom of Bawok-Banganté, founded in 1907 with the help of the friendly Bali-Nyonga kingdom. It is an enclave in the Bali kingdom (*fondom* or kingdom)

Bayangam   Bamileké settlement and kingdom in the Mifi Division, West Region.

Bazou   Bamileké kingdom in Nde Division, West Region.

Beti   Diminutive of Beti-Pahuin. It is also a subdivision of the Beti-Pahuin group of languages and is broken down further into Ewondo, Eton, Bane, Mbida-Mbane and Mvog-Nyenge.

Beti-Pahuin

Diminuted or shortened to Beti, this group of related peoples constitutes the third principal ethnic group in Cameroon. The ethnic homeland of the Beti-Pahuin people is in the Center and South Regions, with fringes and enclaves in the East Region. They are Bantu-speaking and comprise the following:

- Beti (Ewondo, Bane, Mbida-Mbane, Mvog-Nyenge, and Eton),
- Fang (Fang proper, Ntumu, Mvae, and Okak)
- Bulu (Bulu, Fong, Mvele, Zaman, Yebekanga, Yengono, Yembama, Yelinda, Yesum, and Yekebolo.)
- Smaller tribes or ethnic groups Pahuinised by the Beti-Pahuins such as the Baka, Bamvele, Manguissa, Yekaba, Evuzok, Batchanga (Tsinga), Omvang, Yetude peoples.

Beti-Pahuin people are also indigenous in Equatorial Guinea, Gabon and The Republic of Congo.

Betiland	The Beti-Pahuin speaking regions of Cameroon (stretches from the southern half of the Center Region, to the central and eastern parts of the South Region and extend as fringes into the Eastern province), Equatorial Guinea (Rio Muni), Gabon (the northern half), The Republic of Congo (the Northwest), and São Tomé and Príncipe.
Biafra	The short-lived Ibo-dominated state that seceded from Nigeria during the 1966–1970 Nigerian Civil War.
Bota	A suburb of Limbe, Fako Division, Southwest Region.
British Cameroons	The western third of the former German Kamerun that fell under British control following the partition of the German colony. It comprised British Northern Cameroons and British Southern Cameroons.
Boumnyebel	A Bassa village in Nyong and Kelle Division, Center Region.
British Northern Cameroons	The Northern half of British Cameroons that voted to unite with

	Nigeria in 1961, following the controversial United Nations plebiscite in the territory.
British Southern Cameroons	The Southern half of British Cameroons. Became part of the Cameroon Federation in 1961 following a plebiscite that resulted in its reunification with the former French Cameroun. It comprises the Northwest and Southwest Regions of Cameroon.
Buea	The capital town of the Southwest Region and former capital of German Kamerun.
Bulu	One of the peoples of the Beti-Fang ethnic group with a homeland in the South Region.
Cameroonian Pidgin	Also called Cameroonian Creole or Kamtok, it is the Pidgin English spoken in Cameron. It has five variants.
CDU (Cameroon Democratic Union). Called *UDC (Union Démocratique du*	A political party in Cameroon founded by Adamou Ndam Njoya, a former minister of the Ahmadou Ahidjo regime.

Cameroun) in French

| CENER | (*Center National des Etudes et de Recherché*)—Acronym of Cameroon's secret intelligence service (National Center for Studies and Research)—that was changed in 1984 to *Direction Générale de la Recherché Extérieures (*DGRE)—General Directorate for External Research. |

Center Region — Central province of Cameroon. Comprises eight divisions.

CNU (Cameroon National Union) called in French UNC *(Union Nationale Camerounaise)* — Party formed in 1966 from the merger of the political parties operating in Cameroon. It was headed by first Cameroonian president Ahmadou Ahidjo.

CPDM (Cameroon People's Democratic Movement), called in French RDPC *(Rassemblement Démocratique du Peuple Camerounais*) — The CNU renamed in 1985. This is the party in Cameroon. Its former name (1966-1985) was the Cameroon National Union (UNC), which itself was formed in 1966 by the merger of political parties in Cameroon. Before that, it was called the UC (*Union Camerounaise*)---Cameroonian Union (CU), the former political party founded by Ahmadou Ahidjo, the

	former President of the Republic of Cameroon. The CPDM/CNU/CU/UC has been the ruling party since the so-called 'independence of Cameroon in 1960. Paul Biya is the party's president.
CU (Cameroonian Union) called in French *UC (Union Camerounaise)*	Party formed by Ahmadou Ahidjo.
Douala	Largest city, economic capital and capital of Wouri division and Littoral Region.
Duala	A Bantu-speaking people of the Sawabantu subgroup, they are the principal ethnic group of the Wouri Division and the Douala area.
East Cameroon	The French-speaking federal unit of Cameroon from 1961–72. It was formed from the former French Cameroun.
East Region	The Southeastern half of Cameroon. The East Region has four divisions with Bertoua as its capital.

Eton

One of the peoples of the Beti-Fang ethnic group. Found in the Center Region.

Ewondo

One of the peoples of the Beti-Fang group. Found in the Center Region of Cameroon.

Extreme North

A province in the far North of Cameroon. It comprises six divisions.

Free French Forces

These were French and Francophone fighters who continued fighting the axis powers of Germany, Italy, and Japan, even after France surrendered and signed an armistice agreement with Nazi Germany in June 1940. It was formed by General Charles De Gaulle, who was a member of the French cabinet on an official visit to Britain at the time of the surrender. General Charles De Gaulle strongly opposed French capitulation and the armistice signed by the new regime led by Marshall Petain that created the Vichy regime in the South of France, thereby allowing the North of the country to be under German occupation. He urged resistance against German control of France and its collaborationist Vichy puppets. The movement drew recruits mostly from the French empire, especially from French Central Africa, of which French Cameroun was the base at the time, under the new governorship of Jacques Philippe LeClerc. Philippe LeClerc led the Free French Forces' first major victory in the war with the capture in 1941 of Kufra, a town in the then Italian colony of Libya. It incorporated forces of the former Vichy regime in the colonies from 1943 and saw its ranks swollen by Frenchmen after the D-Day landing. The Free French Forces achieved their greatest glory with the liberation of Paris in August 1944, led by the French 2nd Armored Division because it had the least number of blacks in its ranks. By the end of the war, The Free French Movement constituted the fourth largest military force in Europe, fighting against the Axis powers. The right-wing political parties in France have been dominated by its members and the ideology of its founder called Gaullism.

FSD (Front Social- The political party that is described as

Démocrate). The SDF (Social Democratic Front) in French.

the opposition leader in Cameroon. The SDF is led since its inception on May 26, 1990, by John Fru Ndi.

Fulfulde (Fula, Pulaar, Pular, Peul)

A Sene-Gambian language spoken by the Fulani people.

Fulani (Fulani, Fula, Fellata or Peul)

A mixed Negro-Tuareg people inhabiting the Savannah from Sudan to Sene-Gambia, they comprise three groups namely:

The Mbororo, Bororo, Burure or Abore who are pastoralists.

The Fulanin Gida, Ndoowi'en or Magida, who are fully sedentary communities.

The semi-sedentary Peul people who are agriculturalist and ultimately resume pastoralism, but often form permanent communities.

Foulanis, Fulanis or Peuls are the second most populous ethnic group in Cameroon. Found mostly in the northern provinces of Adamawa, North and Extreme North. Their language is the lingua franca of this part of Cameroon.

Foumbam
The capital of the Noun Division and the Bamounland. Found in the West Region.

Foumbot
Agricultural settlement in the Noun Division.

French Cameroun
The Eastern two third of the former German Kamerun that fell under the control of the French following the partition of the German colony by Britain and France. It became a French mandatory territory and later trust territory from 1918–1960.

Garoua
The capital of the North Region and Benue Division.

Graffi
Pidgin German word for a grass field. A name often applied collectively to the semi-Bantu peoples of the Northwest and West Regions of Cameroon.

Graffiland
Cameroonian word for Western High Plateau, Western Highlands, or Bamenda Grassfields. Mountainous grassland region of the Northwest and West Regions of Cameroon. It

comprises the Bamilekéland and Bamounland in the south, and the Ngembaland, Chambaland, and Tikarland in the north.

Ibo

One of the four principal ethnic groups of Nigeria. Found in the southeast.

Idenau

A town in Fako Division, Southwest Region.

Kamveu

The local council of notables among the different Bamileké kingdoms.

Koufra (Kufra)

An important but isolated Oasis settlement in the southeastern Libyan desert that was of strategic importance for the North African campaign during the Second World War. Its capture from the Italians by the Free French Forces marked the first major battle won by France in the war, thereby boosting General Charles De Gaulle's prestige and the morale of the demoralized anti-Vichy forces.

Koutaba

A settlement in the Bamounland, Noun Division, West Region. Also a major military and air base in

Cameroon,

Kumba	The largest city in the Southwest Region and capital of Meme Division. It is located about 70 miles north of Limbe.
KNDP (Cameroon National Democratic Party)	Nationalist party in British Cameroons. It led the campaign that realized the reunification of British Southern Cameroons with former French Cameroun.
Limbe	Former Victoria. It is the capital of Fako Division in the Southwest Region.
Littoral	Coastal province of Cameroon. It consists of four divisions.
Loum	An agricultural town in the Mungo Division, in the north of the Littoral Region.
Maguida (Magida)	Name erroneously used for the peoples of the Moslem North that originated from the third group of Fulanis—the Fulanin Gida, comprising the fully sedentary Fulani communities.

Mamfe

The capital of Manyu Division in the Southwest Region.

Manjibo

A Bamoun village in the Noun Division.

Mankon

Mankon is a Ngemba kingdom and part of the city of Bamenda.

Maroua

The capital of the Extreme North Region and Diamare Division.

Mayo Tsanaga

A division in the Extreme North Region of Cameroon.

Mayo Tsava

A division in the Extreme North Region of Cameroon.

Mbengwi

The capital of Momo Division in the Northwest Region.

Mboh

A Bantu-speaking people of the Mungo Division in the Littoral Region, with fringes of their homeland in the Southwest and Western provinces.

Mokolo	Capital of Mayo Tsanaga Division.
Molyko	A suburb of Buea in the Southwest Region.
Mora	The capital of Mayo Tsava Division.
Mutengene	A junction town to Limbe, Buea, and Tiko, in Fako Division, Southwest Region.
Nde	Formerly called Banganté Division. It is found in the West Region of Cameroon.
Ngaoundéré	Capital of the Vina Division and Adamawa Region.
Ngemba	The second most populous peoples of the semi-Bantu group. The Ngemba peoples are found in the northern half of the Cameroon Grassland (Western Highlands), mostly in the Mezam and Momo Divisions of the Northwest Region. The Ngemba people related dialects.
Ngembaland	The Southwestern part of the Northwest Region that is composed of

	several traditional kingdoms or fondoms speaking closely related dialects.
Nkongsamba	The capital of the Mungo Division of Cameroon. It is also the largest city in the area.
Nkwen	A traditional Ngemba kingdom and part of the city of Bamenda.
North Region	Central of the Grand North Regions. It comprises four divisions.
Northwest Region	A province from the former Federal unit of West Cameroon and the former territory of British Southern Cameroons. Peopled by semi-Bantu groups of Tikar, Ngemba and Chamba speakers. Their compatriots in the Southwest Region collectively call them 'Graffis'.
NUDP (National Union for Democracy and Progress) Called UNDP *(Union Nationale pour la Démocratie et le Progrès)* in French	A political party in Cameroon founded by Samuel Eboua, a former minister of the regime Ahmadou Ahidjo. Bello Bouba Maigari, a former prime minister of the Biya regime, usurped the leadership of the party and has been its president since 1992.

Nzui-Mantor	Banganté-Bamileké word for the panther or leopard.
OK (One Cameroon)	An offshoot of the UPC after it was also banned in British Cameroons.
Peul	A French term for Fulani borrowed from the Wolof language.
RDPC (Rassemblement Démocratique du Peuple Camerounais), Called CPDM (Cameroon People's Democratic Movement) in English	The party in power in Cameroon. CNU renamed in 1985.
SDF (Social Democratic Front) or *FSD (Front Social-Démocrate)* in French	The political party that is described as the opposition leader in Cameroon. The SDF is led since its inception on May 26, 1990, by John Fru Ndi.
Semi-Bantu	The unique and unrelated peoples in Africa, comprising the Bamileké, Bamoun, Tikar, Ngemba and Chamba peoples.

Sokolo	A suburb in Limbe, Southwest Region.
South Region	Cameroon's southern coastal province. It comprises the three divisions of Ntem, Ocean and Dja and Lobo.
Southwest Region	Southwestern coastal province of Cameroon. It has four divisions. Formerly a part of British Southern Cameroons and the federal unit of West Cameroon.
Tcholliré	The capital of Rey Bouba Division in the North Region.
Tiko	A coastal town in Fako Division in the Southwest Region.
Tonga	Bamileké settlement and kingdom in the Nde Division, West Region.
Tuareg	A Berber-speaking people of the Mazigh group inhabiting the central Sahara from Southern Algeria and Tripolitania in Libya, to the middle Niger and the northern borders of Nigeria. They moved to the interior of the Sahara Desert to escape the Arab invasion of North Africa in the 7th and

8th century.

UDC (Union Démocratique du Cameroun) or CDU (Cameroon Democratic Union) in English — A political party in Cameroon founded by Adamou Ndam Njoya, former minister of the Ahmadou Ahidjo regime.

UNC (Union Nationale du Cameroun). Called CNU (Cameroon National Union) in English — Party formed in 1966 from the merger of political parties operating in Cameroon. It was headed by the first Cameroonian president Ahmadou Ahidjo.

UNDP (Union Nationale pour la Démocratie et le Progrès) or National Union for Democracy and Progress (NUDP) in English — A political party in Cameroon founded by Samuel Eboua, former minister of the regime Ahmadou Ahidjo. Bello Bouba Maigari, a former prime minister of the Biya regime, usurped the leadership of the party and has been its president since 1992.

UPC (Union of the Populations of the Cameroons) — First national and nationalistic party in Cameroon. The historic UPC was formed in 1948. Banned in 1955, it resorted to an armed struggle that continued well into the late 1960s.

Victoria

Former name of Limbe. Was founded in 1857 by missionaries for the settlement of rescued or freed slaves.

West Region

The southern half of the Western Highlands of Cameroon. It is populated by the Bamileké and Bamoun peoples. It is also Cameroon's cultural and agricultural heartland, and is remembered for its historic role as the center of the country's nationalism and liberation struggle against the French Army in the land. It comprises the six divisions of Bamboutous, Menoua, Mifi, Nde, Noun, and Upper Nkam.

Wolowose

Cameroonian word for a whore.

Wum

The capital of Menchum Division in the Northwest Region.

Yaoundé

Cameroon's second largest city and national capital. Also the capital of the Center Region and Nfoundi Division.